BLUEPRINTS
Science
Key Stage 1
Copymasters

Third edition

Jim Fitzsimmons

Rhona Whiteford

Stanley Thornes (Publishers) Ltd

Stanley Thornes for TEACHERS:
BLUEPRINTS • PRIMARY COLOURS • LEARNING TARGETS

Stanley Thornes for Teachers publishes practical teacher's ideas books and photocopiable resources for use in primary schools. Our three key series, **Blueprints**, **Primary Colours** and **Learning Targets** together provide busy teachers with unbeatable curriculum coverage, inspiration and value for money. We mail teachers and schools about our books regularly. To join the mailing list simply photocopy and complete the form below and return using the **FREEPOST** address to receive regular updates on our new and existing titles. You may also like to add the name of a friend who would be interested in being on the mailing list. Books can be bought by credit card over the telephone and information obtained on (01242) 267280.

Please add my name to the *Stanley Thornes for* **TEACHERS** mailing list.

Mr/Mrs/Miss/Ms _____

Address _____

_____ postcode _____

School address _____

_____ postcode _____

Please also send information about *Stanley Thornes for* **TEACHERS** to:

Mr/Mrs/Miss/Ms _____

Address _____

_____ postcode _____

To: Marketing Services Dept., Stanley Thornes Ltd, FREEPOST (GR 782), Cheltenham, GL50 1BR

First published in 1990 as Blueprints Science 5–7 Copymasters
Second edition published in 1992.
Third edition published in 1995.
First published in new binding in 1997 by:
Stanley Thornes (Publishers) Ltd

Reprinted in 2002 by:
Nelson Thornes Ltd
Delta Place
27 Bath Road
Cheltenham GL53 7TH
United Kingdom

A catalogue record for this book is available from the British Library.

ISBN 0–7487–3449–X

Typeset by Tech-Set Ltd.
Printed and bound in Great Britain by The Bath Press

02 03 04 05 06 / 10 9 8 7 6 5 4

CONTENTS

Contents

Record sheets 1–6

INTRODUCTION

In this book there are 97 photocopiable copymasters linked to many of the activities in the Teacher's Resource Book. Where the copymasters are referred to in the text of the Teacher's Resource Book there are some instructions on how to use them. They are referred to by number in the Teacher's Resource Book by this symbol: . The copymasters give the children a chance to record activities and results in an organised way, and in some cases to consolidate learning that has gone before. When the children have completed these copymasters they can be added to workfiles or used as exemplar material in pupil profiles. You may also wish to use completed copymasters as a resource for your assessments. There are six record sheets at the back of this book, on which you can note which copymasters the children have made use of, and their experience of work contributing to the sections of the Programme of Study for National Curriculum Science.

At the top of each copymaster you will find symbols that explain how that sheet contributes to work on the all important Experimental and Investigative Science section of the Programme of Study. These symbols are explained in detail in the Teacher's Resource Book, but they are set out here for easy reference.

Level 1

 Observation   Discussion   Measure   Record findings   Communication   Drawing tables and charts   Comparing   Health and safety reminder   Ask questions

Level 2

 Observation   Discussion   Measure   Record findings   Communication   Drawing tables and charts   Ask questions   Comparing   Identify

 Interpret findings   Formulate hypotheses   Interpret and generalise   Health and safety reminder

Level 3

 Observation   Discussion   Measure   Record findings   Communication   Drawing tables and charts   Comparing   Identify   Fair/unfair test

 Formulate hypotheses   Interpret and generalise   Support prediction   Interpret findings   Health and safety reminder

Name _____

My favourite TV programme

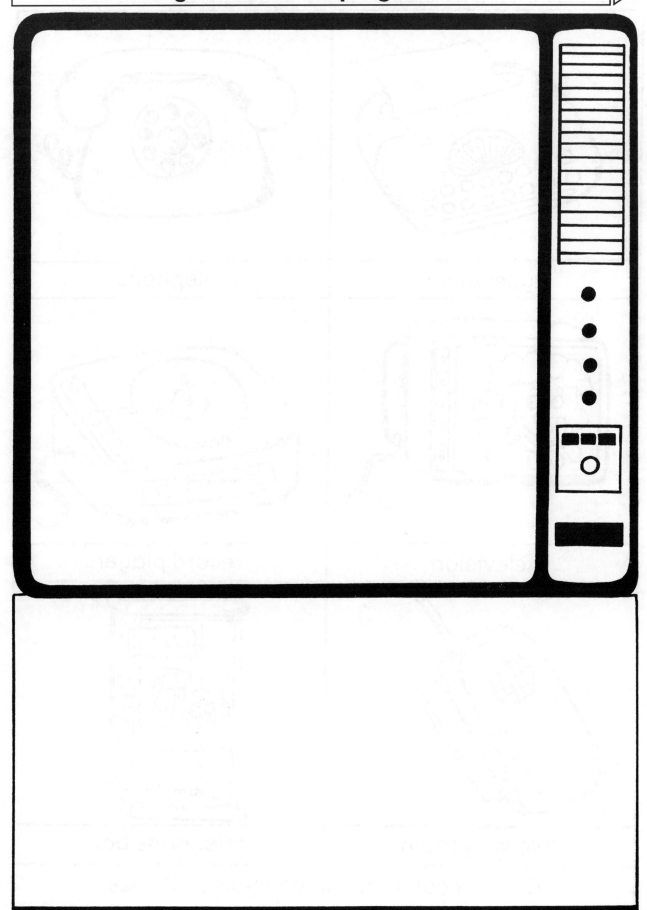

Talking to someone a long way away

typewriter

telephone

television

record player

two-way radio

telephone box

Circle or colour the things you could use.

I spy aerials

I can see ☐ aerials.

Passing on visual information

Have you seen or used these things?

Let's play I-spy

	Television	Yes	No
	Place		
	Date		

	Computer	Yes	No
	Place		
	Date		

	Video	Yes	No
	Place		
	Date		

	Teletext	Yes	No
	Place		
	Date		

	Motorway warning light	Yes	No
	Place		
	Date		

BBC Ceefax

DAYTIME

100 News
200 Sports
300 City
400 Breakfast
500 Travel
600 T.V. & radio

Passing on audio information

Have you seen or used these things?

Have you?

	Radio	Yes	No
	Place		
	Date		
	Tape recorder	Yes	No
	Place		
	Date		
	Record player	Yes	No
	Place		
	Date		
	CD player	Yes	No
	Place		
	Date		
	Telephone	Yes	No
	Place		
	Date		

Storing information

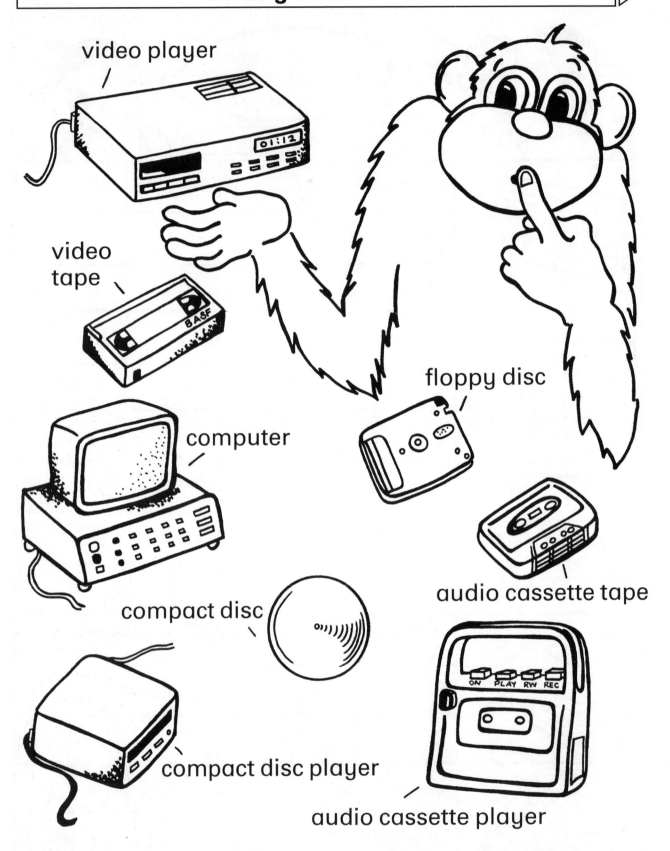

video player

video tape

floppy disc

computer

audio cassette tape

compact disc

compact disc player

audio cassette player

Match the machine to the disc or tape it uses.

Using a tape recorder

Making a recording: Number the correct order.

Check microphone	Press play	Stop

Press 'record'	Plug in/Switch on	Make recording

Insert tape correctly	Rewind	Listen to recording

   123=

What shall I wear?

A day out

Weather record

Monday			
Tuesday			
Wednesday			
Thursday			
Friday			

The seasons

Draw yourself having fun in each season of the year.
Make sure you are wearing the proper clothes.

Hot and cold

The seasons clock

What would you wear in the different seasons?

W _ _ _ _ _

S _ _ _ _ _

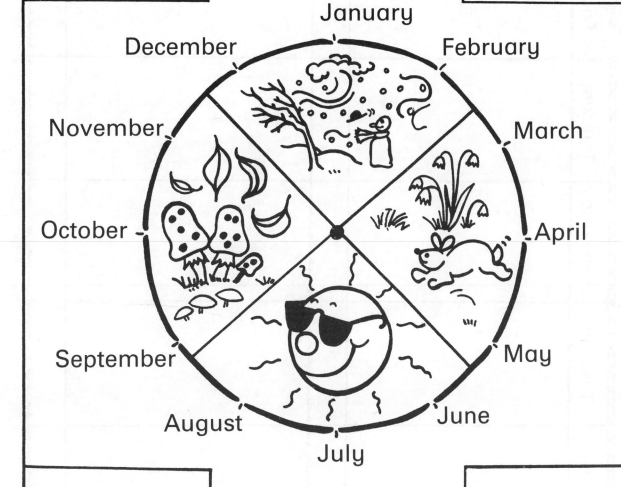

A _ _ _ _ _

S _ _ _ _ _

| Winter | Spring | Summer | Autumn |

Weather record

Weather record

	Sunday	Monday	Tuesday	Wednesday	Thursday	Friday	Saturday
Morning							
Temperature							
Afternoon							
Temperature							

Name _____

Shall I play outside?

Draw yourself playing outside in these temperatures.

Draw in the mercury on the thermometer.

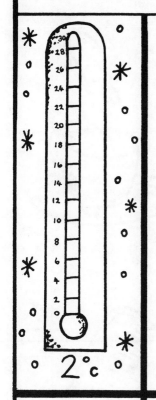

2°c

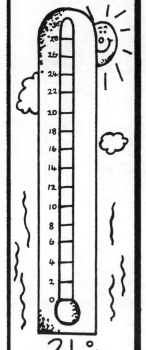

24°c

Name _____

Living and non-living

Make a set of the drawings of living things and colour them in.

Name _____

Things I do with my body

writing

reading

dancing

swimming

painting

running

listening

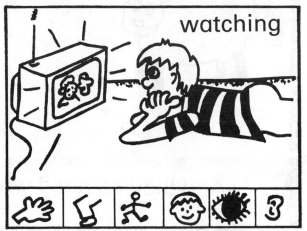

watching

All living things need food

Match the animal with its food.

And they **all** need water.

Diary

1.

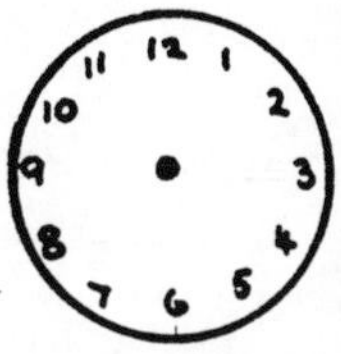

Date _____

2.

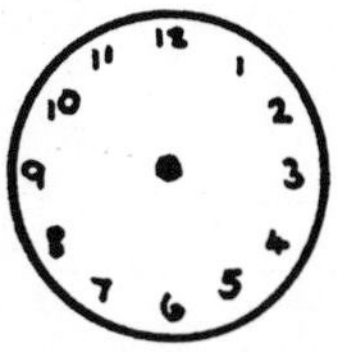

Date _____

3.

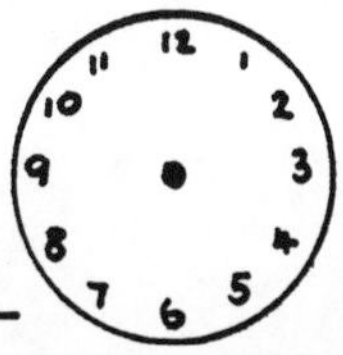

Date _____

4.

Date _____

5.

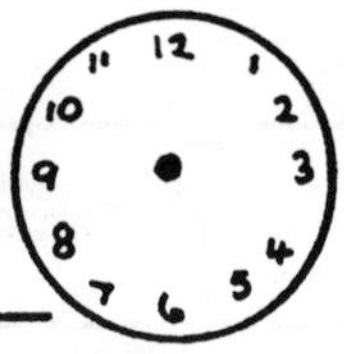

Date _____

6.

Date _____

My day

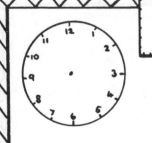

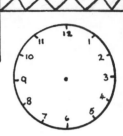

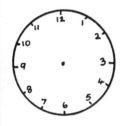

In the morning I _____

At lunch-time I _____

In the afternoon I _____

In the evening I _____

Copymaster 20

What is it?

This is a

Feeding	**Breathing**
Movement	**Behaviour**

Habitat

ST. MARY'S UNIVERSITY COLLEGE
A COLLEGE OF THE QUEEN'S UNIVERSITY OF BELFAST

Copymaster 21

Can you match the families?

c _ _ _	l _ _ _	b _ _ _
e _ _	f _ _ _	h _ _
c _ _ _ _ _	m _ _ _	r _ _ _
c _ _ _	c _ _ _ _	s _ _ _ _ _ _ _ _

Horses	Cattle	Chickens	Sheep
stallion	bull	cock	ram
mare	cow	hen	ewe
foal	calf	chick	lamb
red	blue	yellow	green

Copymaster 22

Mr Litter

Colour the things you found.

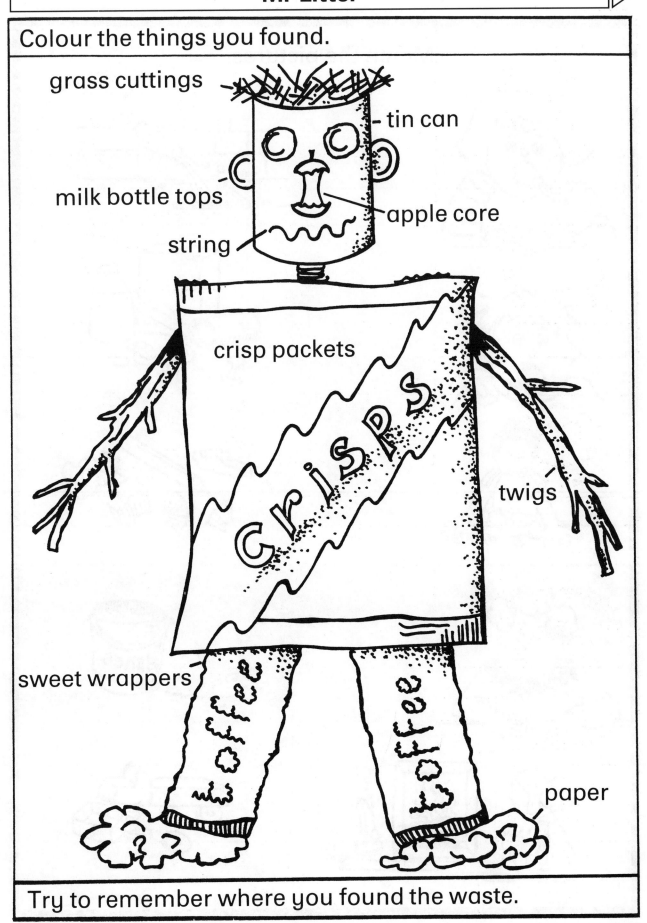

grass cuttings

tin can

milk bottle tops

string

apple core

crisp packets

CRISPS

twigs

sweet wrappers

toffee

toffee

paper

Try to remember where you found the waste.

Where did it come from?

Match the pictures.

Where is it?

HIG SONS LTD.

Draw a ring around the waste.

Rubbish collection

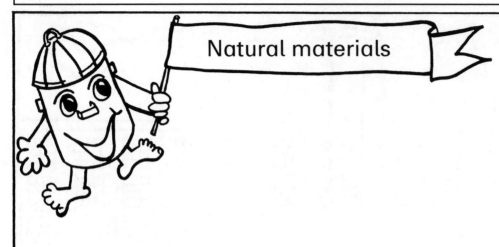

Natural materials

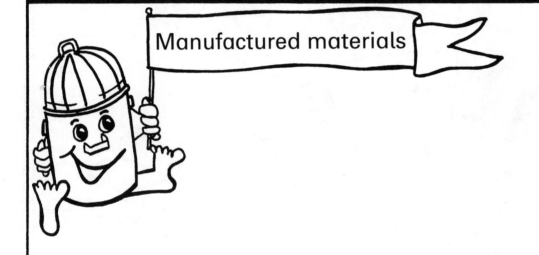

Manufactured materials

Mixtures

What rots?

The material tested

This material was put in these places.

Place	Week 1	Week 2	Week 3
In the air outside			
In the air inside			
In water			
In garden soil			
In sand			
In wet peat			

Rainbow body

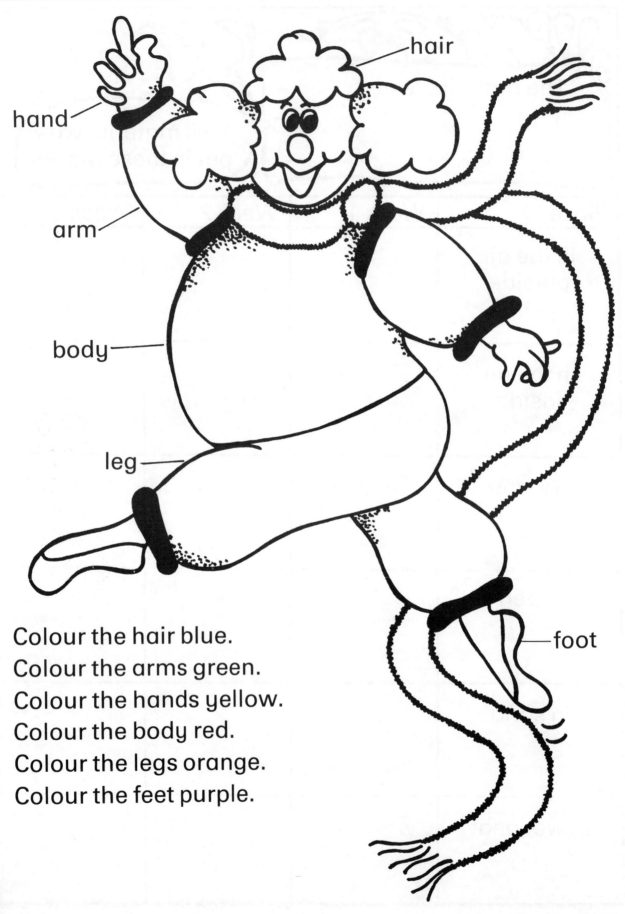

Colour the hair blue.
Colour the arms green.
Colour the hands yellow.
Colour the body red.
Colour the legs orange.
Colour the feet purple.

We are what we eat

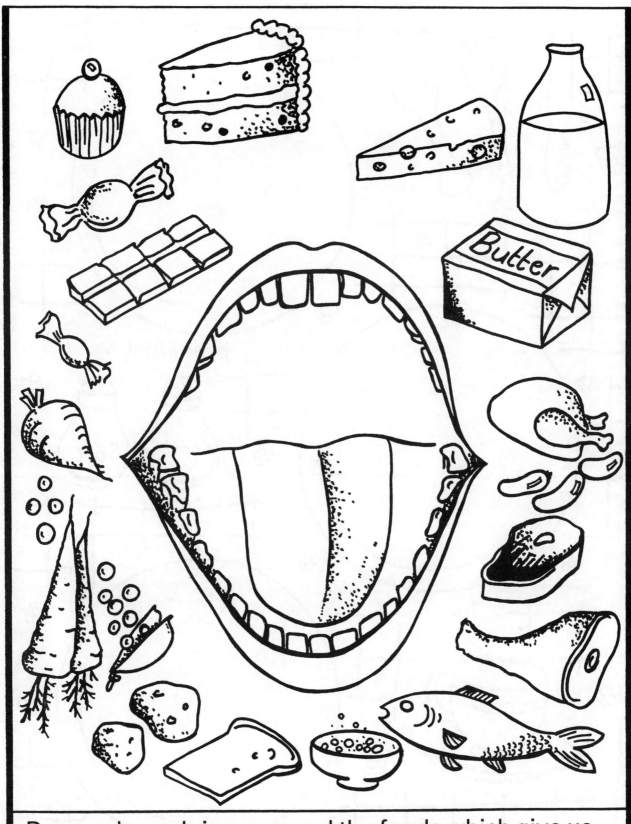

Draw coloured rings around the foods which give us
energy (red), build our bodies (blue), clean us out
(green).

       Copymaster 29

Name _____

The food we eat

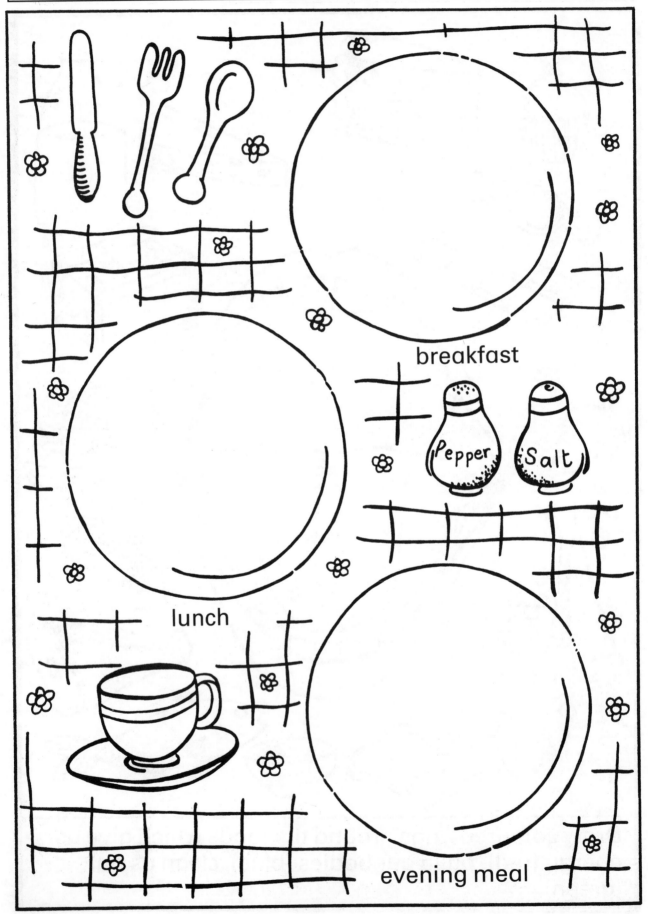

breakfast

lunch

Pepper   Salt

evening meal

Taking care of yourself

Name of person?

Food	What foods do you usually have for:
	breakfast _____
	lunch _____
	tea _____
	supper _____

Sleep	What time do you go to bed? _____
	What time do you get up? _____
	How many hours' sleep do you have each night? hours

Exercise

Tick if you do these things in the week.

walk	run	skip	play

ride a bike	skate	swim

play football	ride a horse	others

Hygiene

Number of washes each day

Number of times teeth cleaned each day

Number of baths in a week

I think I am 😊 I am not 😟 healthy.

Name _____

What do plants need?

Write what happened.

soil, no water, no light 	
soil, water, no light 	
soil, water, light 	
water, light, no soil 	

Name _____

Plants

Write the names of the different parts of the plants.

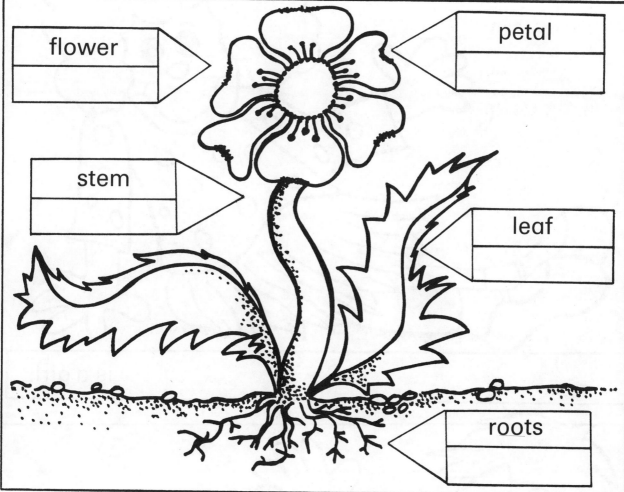

flower

petal

stem

leaf

roots

Finish off the picture.

Copymaster 33

Name _____

Are you a boy or a girl?

is a girl.

is a boy.

Faces

This is me.

People

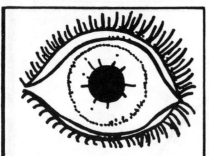

My eyes are

My hair is

My skin is

This is me.

These people live in my house.

Things I am good at

Colour or circle the activities you can do.

Name _____

All about me

Name	Age	Sex

Place of birth

Height	cm	Weight	kg

Colour of eyes _____

Colour of skin _____

Colour of hair _____

Shoe size

Other facts

Elements of a graph

I can do this

I am ____ cm tall.

I can reach up to ____ cm.

I can leap up to ____ cm.

I can jump ____ cm.

I can stand on one leg for

____ minutes and ____ seconds.

Our walk

On our walk

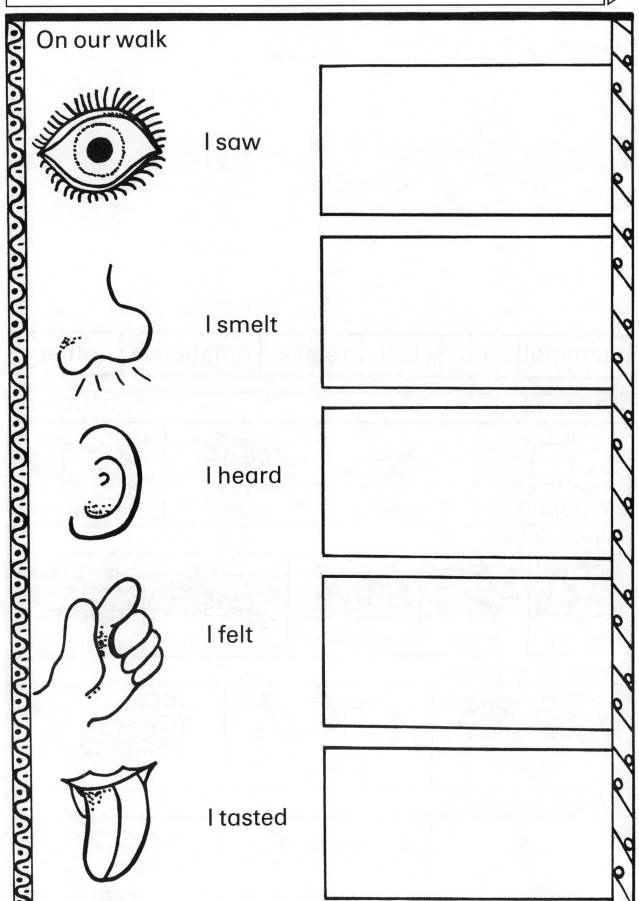

I saw

I smelt

I heard

I felt

I tasted

What do animals need?

This is a _____

mammal	bird	fish	reptile	amphibian	other

What it likes

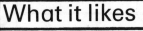

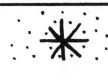

warmth	cold	light	dark

Where it lives

mountain	plain	jungle/wood	underground	underwater

What food it likes

plants	animals	both

Who it lives with

alone	family	herd

Copymaster 42

Name _____

Caring for pets ▷

This is my pet _____

water

feeding

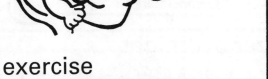

exercise

cleaning out

grooming

training and play

Copymaster 43

Changes

Write and draw
what happened.

We put the seedlings in a hot oven.

Temperature [   ] °C

We put the seedlings on a table in our classroom.

Temperature [   ] °C

We put the seedlings in the freezer overnight.

Temperature [   ] °C

Copymaster 44

Our neighbourhood

Human activity	How these activities affect our neighbourhood
Industry	
Agriculture	
Mining	
Houses	
Parks	
Motorways	
Airports	
Cars	
Oil refinery/ power stations	
Reservoirs	
Other	

Materials I found

This is smooth.

This is rough.

This is hard.

This is soft.

This is bumpy.

This is spongy.

This is slippery.

This is sticky.

This is squashy.

Look at shapes

Finish off the picture.

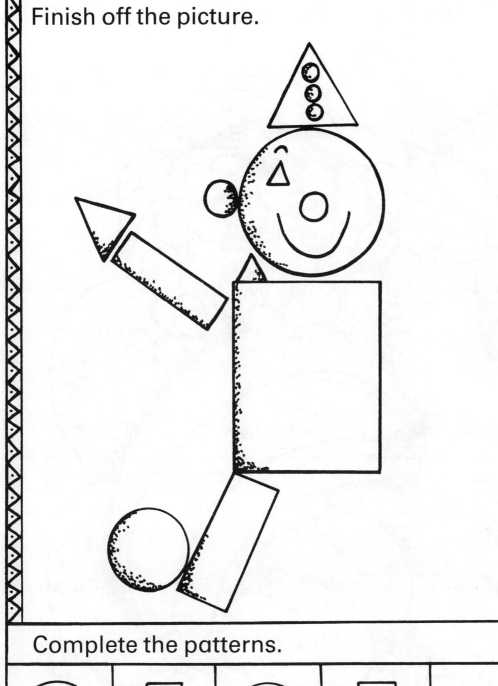

Complete the patterns.

Fruit colours

Colour these fruits.

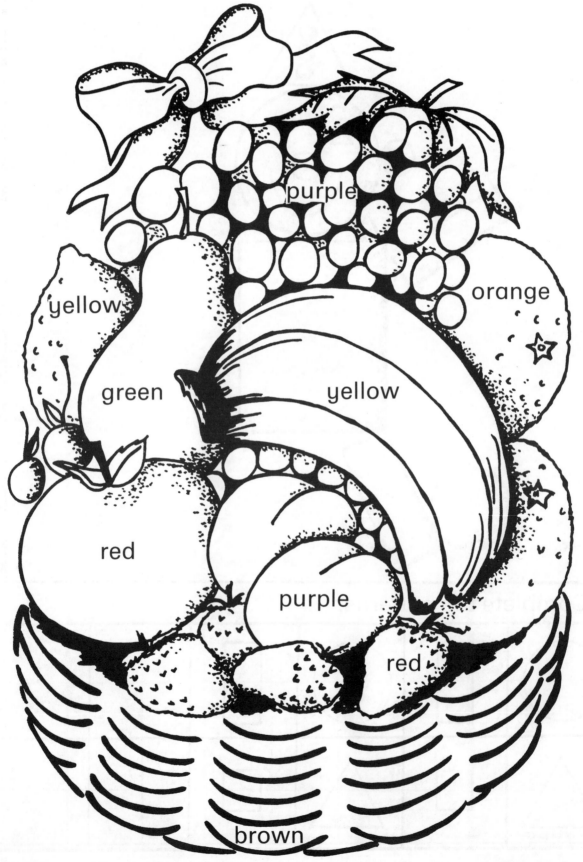

Looking at materials

Properties	The materials we looked at						
	iron	rock	glass	wood	paper	fabric	plastic
hard							
soft							
rough							
smooth							
rigid							
flexible							
shiny							
dull							
transparent							
translucent							
opaque							
fixed shape							
malleable							
bounces							
does not bounce							

Name _____

Comparing materials

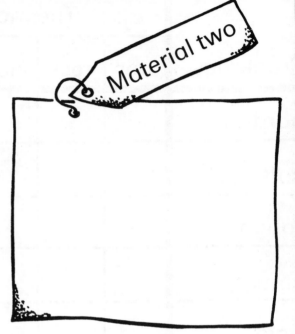

Differences	Similarities	Differences

Name _____

What is it?

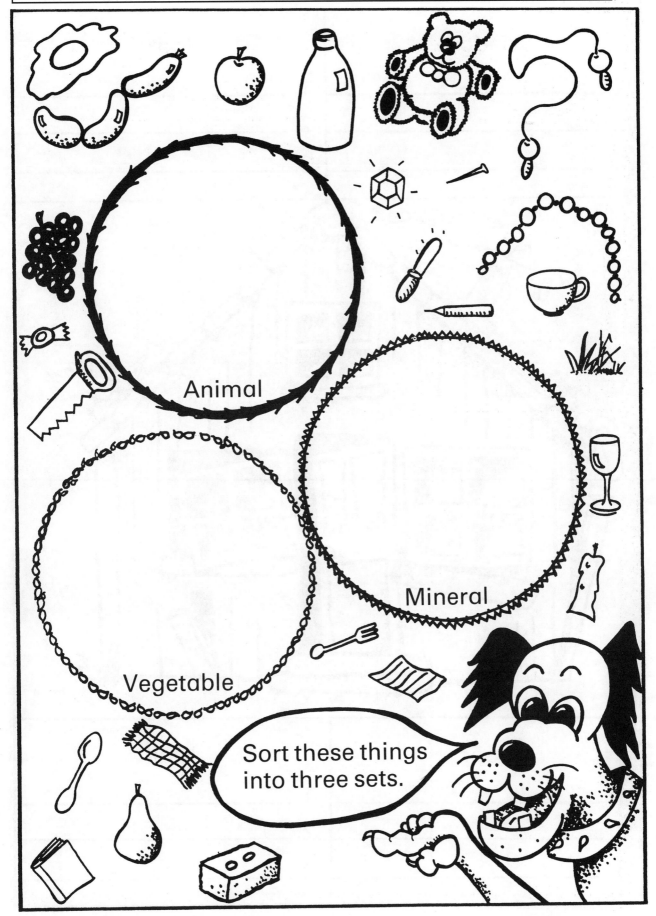

Animal

Mineral

Vegetable

Sort these things into three sets.

Grouping materials

Window

1. _____
2. _____
3. _____

Roof

1. _____
2. _____
3. _____

Door

1. _____
2. _____
3. _____

Wall

1. _____
2. _____
3. _____

Copymaster 52

Weathering

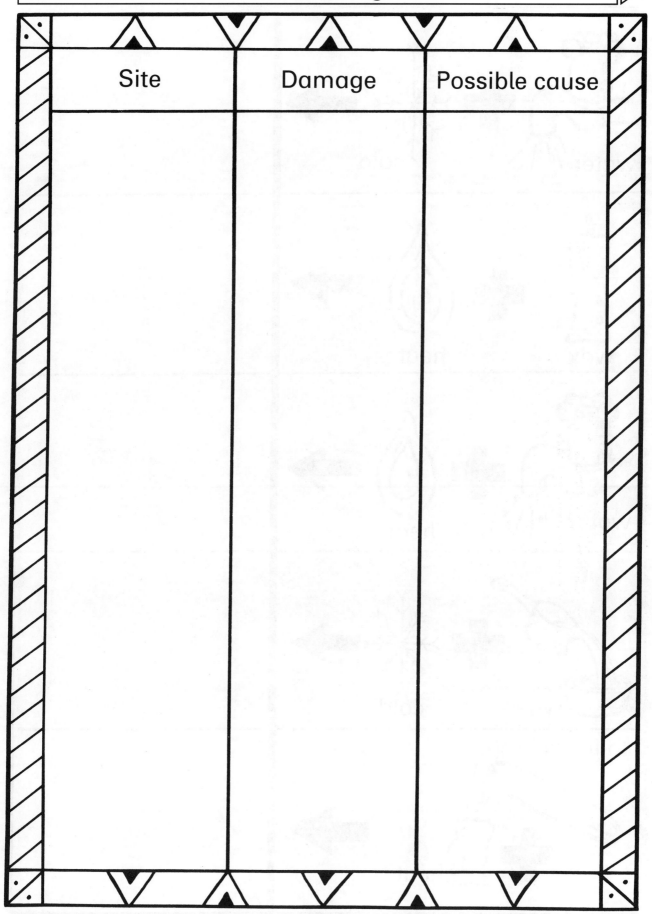

Site	Damage	Possible cause

Changes

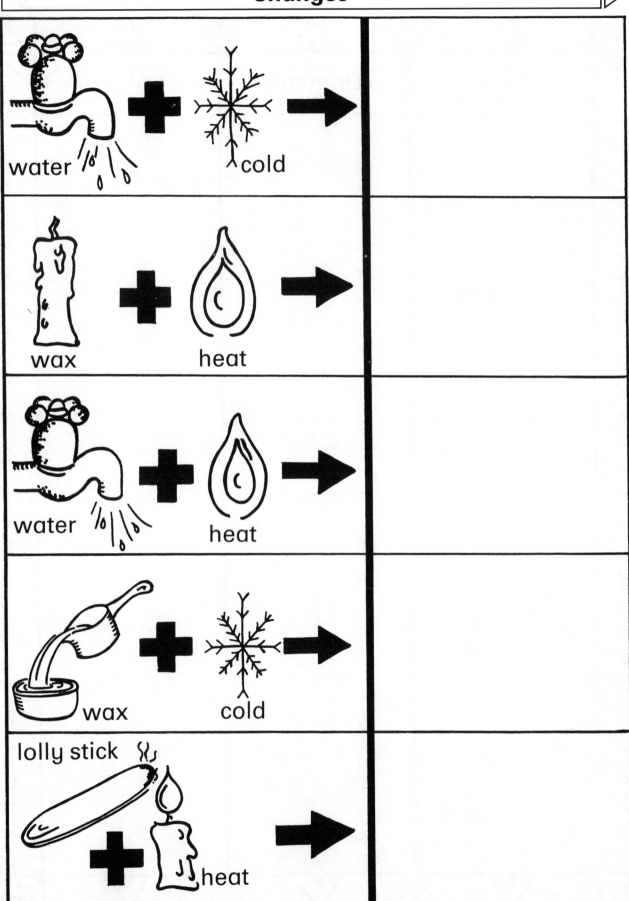

water + cold →

wax + heat →

water + heat →

wax + cold →

lolly stick + heat →

Permanent change

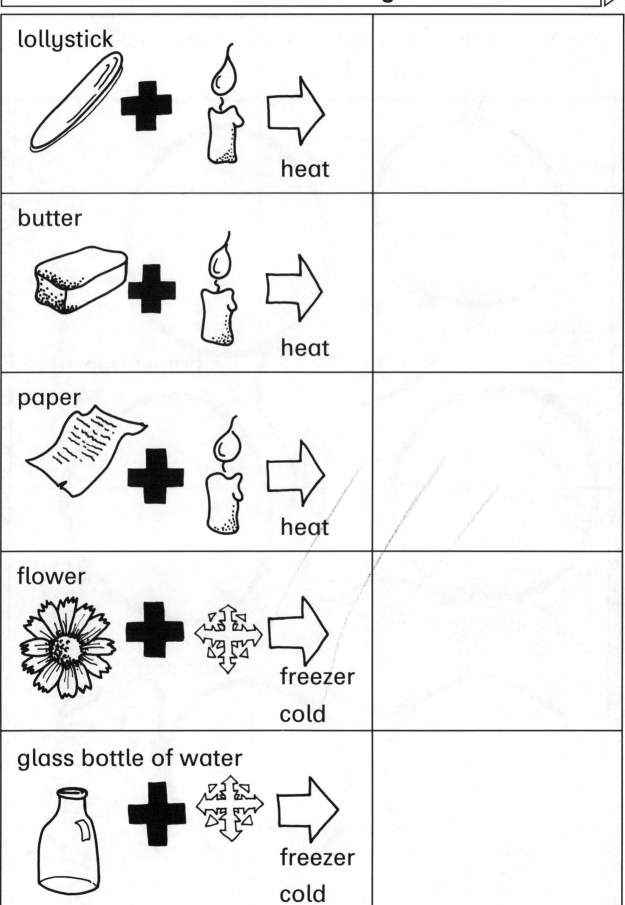

lollystick + candle → heat	
butter + candle → heat	
paper + candle → heat	
flower + freezer cold →	
glass bottle of water + freezer cold →	

Static electricity

I rubbed a balloon on my head. Static electricity on the balloon picked up these things.

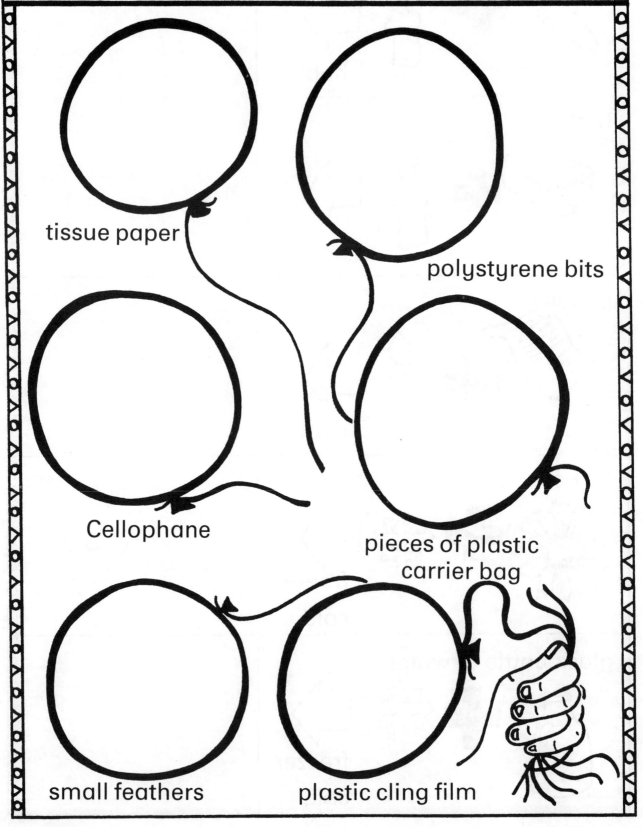

tissue paper

polystyrene bits

Cellophane

pieces of plastic carrier bag

small feathers

plastic cling film

Electrical appliances at home

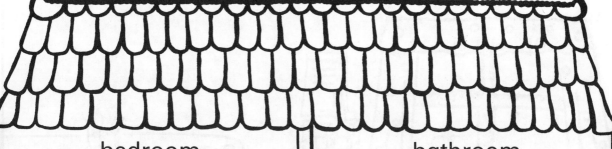

bedroom

bathroom

lounge

kitchen/dining room

Dangers from electricity

Danger

Repair worn flex.

Don't poke in sockets.

Switch off when not in use.

Don't touch electrical things with wet hands.

Don't use electrical equipment in the bathroom.

Don't overload sockets.

Look out for

Join the warning to the correct picture.

Circuits

How did you push these things?

Draw a blue line round the things you pushed with your hand and arm.
Draw a red line round the things you pushed with your leg and foot.
Draw a green line round the things you pushed with your whole body.

The mighty wind race

Sails

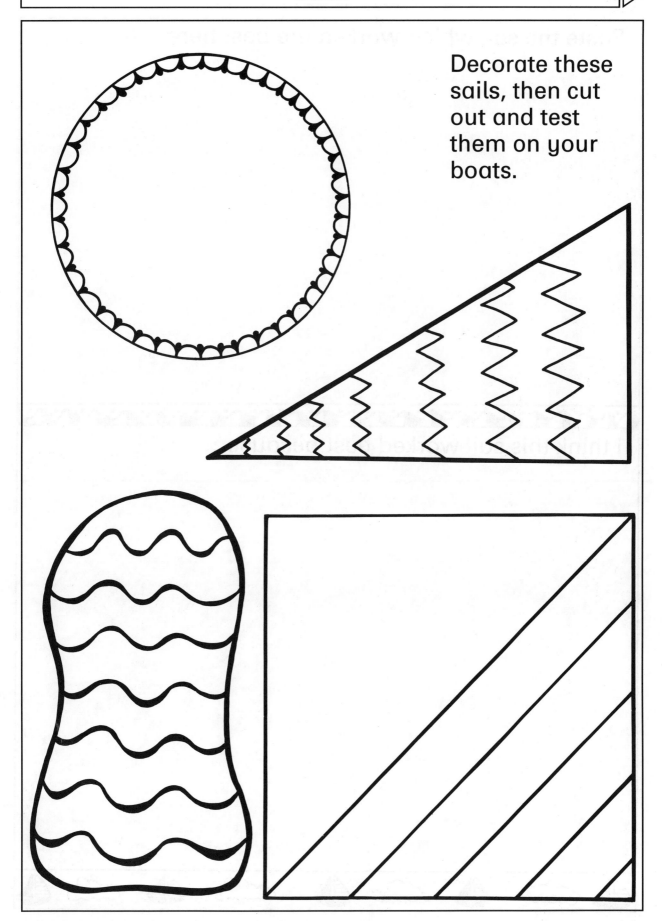

Decorate these sails, then cut out and test them on your boats.

Name _____

Sails test results

Paste the sail which worked the best here.

I think this sail worked best because...

Copymaster 64

Water pushes things

Which of these things could you push with your jet of water?
Tick if the water pushed it.
Cross if the water could not push it.

plastic bucket

feather

ping-pong ball

football

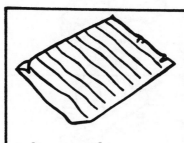

piece of paper

piece of wood

toy car

waste bin

quoit

Pushing and pulling

I do these things when I am:

writing			sweeping floor			riding bicycle		
push	pull	both	push	pull	both	push	pull	both

in a tug of war			rolling a ball			climbing a rope		
push	pull	both	push	pull	both	push	pull	both

I measured the strength of my push and pull.

I pushed against the scales. It showed _____.

I pulled on the spring balance. It showed _____.

Guess what

I guessed which of these things were attracted to a magnet and then I tested them to see if I was correct.

	material	guess	is attracted	is not attracted	
1.					
2.					
3.					
4.					
5.					

Name _____

Magnetic poles

Air is all around

How many things can you see that are moved by air?

| | things |

Draw three things which you play with that are filled with air.

Name _____

Floating and sinking

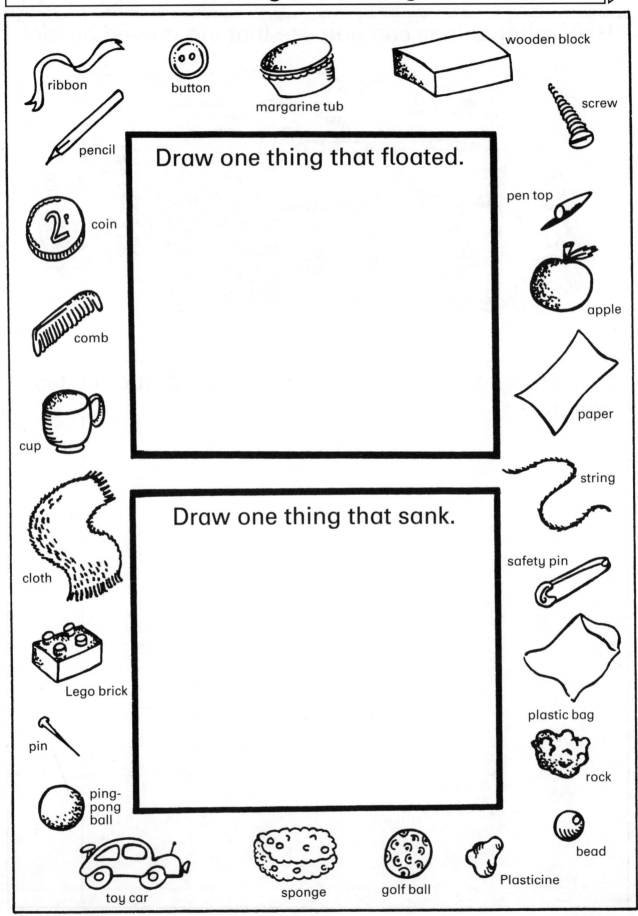

ribbon

button

margarine tub

wooden block

pencil

screw

Draw one thing that floated.

coin

pen top

comb

apple

cup

paper

string

cloth

safety pin

Lego brick

plastic bag

Draw one thing that sank.

pin

rock

ping-pong ball

bead

toy car

sponge

golf ball

Plasticine

How things move when pushed

How things move when pushed		flat surface		downward slope		upward slope	
object		gentle push	strong push	when pushing stopped		distance travelled	
				continued moving	stopped		
toy car							
doll's pram							
skateboard							
tray							
box							
block of wood							

Trying to make objects swerve

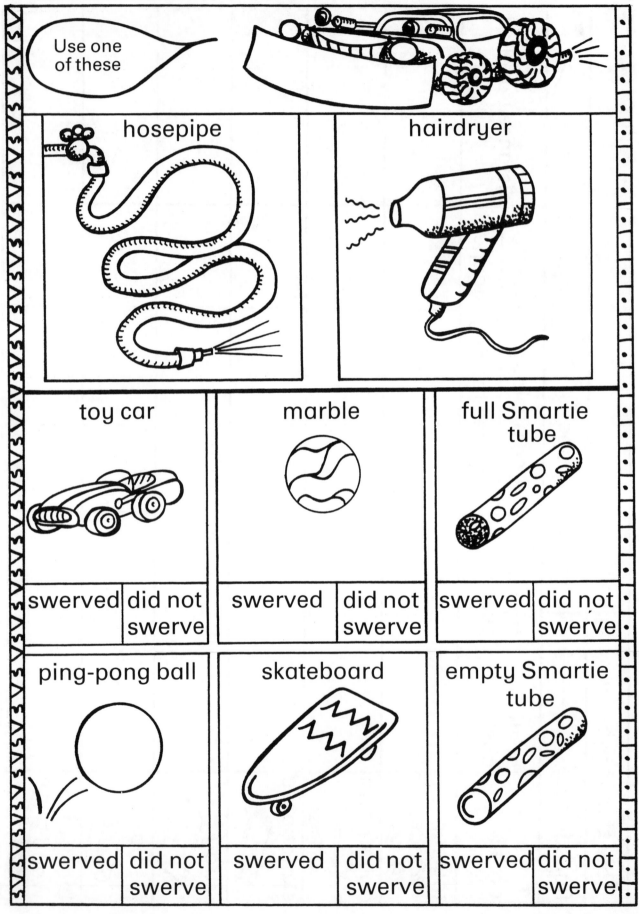

Use one of these

hosepipe	hairdryer

toy car	marble	full Smartie tube
swerved	did not swerve	swerved	did not swerve	swerved	did not swerve

ping-pong ball	skateboard	empty Smartie tube
swerved	did not swerve	swerved	did not swerve	swerved	did not swerve

Copymaster 72

Air power

You will need these things.

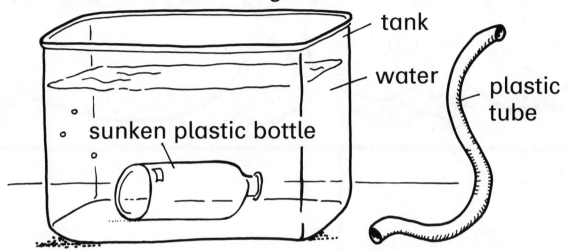

tank

water

plastic tube

sunken plastic bottle

Can you make this bottle float to the surface of the water using air as the force?

Draw or write what you did.

  H **?**

Air

I-spy air!

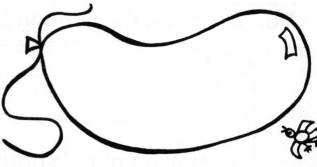

1.	
2.	
3.	
4.	
5.	

The amazing ...

This is what it looks like.

This is how I made it.

I made a ...

I made a

It looks like this.

I used these things to make it.

This is how I made it.

This is what happened when I used it.

This is how it worked.

Lights

Draw a ring around the places where light comes from.

Day

Night

Mixing colours

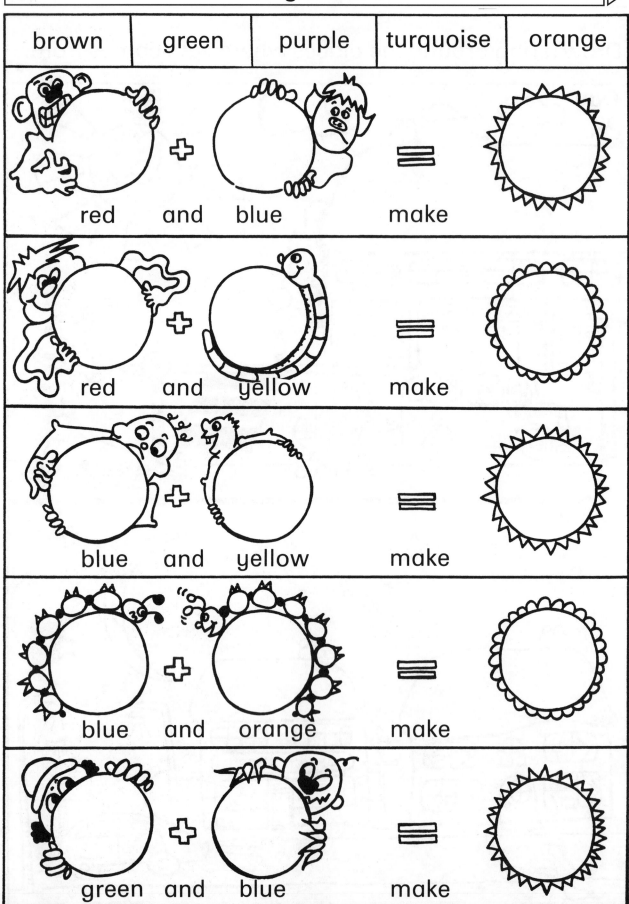

brown	green	purple	turquoise	orange

red and blue make

red and yellow make

blue and yellow make

blue and orange make

green and blue make

Colours in nature

Changes in living things

Match the pictures to the season and complete the word.

| Spring | Summer | Autumn | Winter |

S _ _ _ _ _ _

S _ _ _ _ _ _

W _ _ _ _ _ _

A _ _ _ _ _ _

Using mirrors

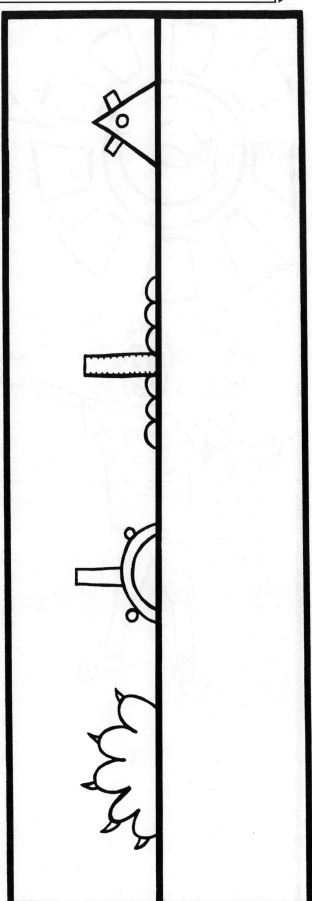

Shadows 1

Name _____

Shadows 2

Get a torch and shine it on a cup in these directions.

Draw in the  where you see it.

 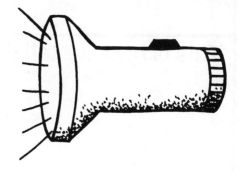

Copymaster 83

Name _____

Making a sundial

We made a sundial.

We used

This is what we did.

This is how we tell the time.

Shades and shadows

Put the sun in the sky and draw the shadows where they should fall. Colour and shade the picture.

Name _____

Now you see it, now you don't

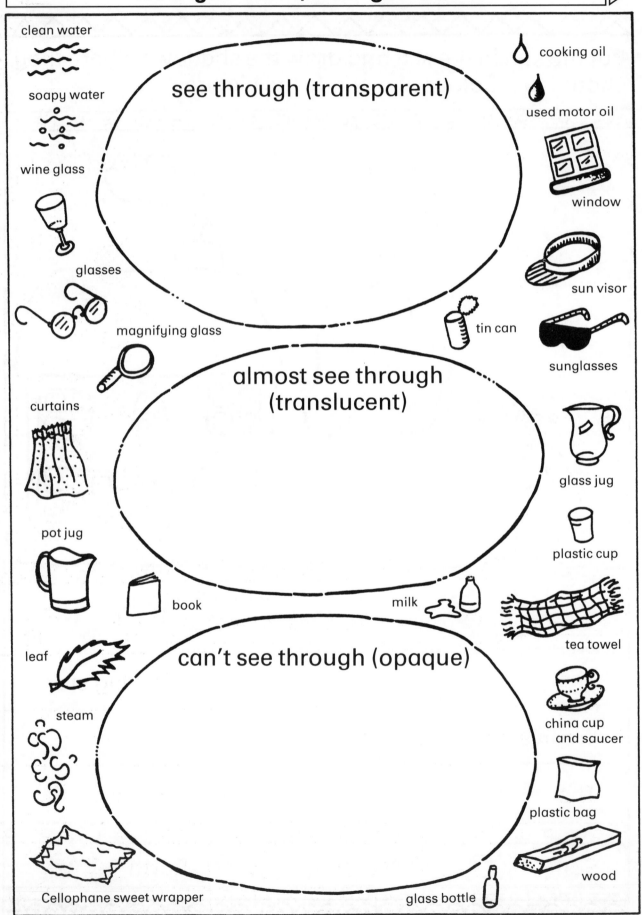

clean water

soapy water

wine glass

glasses

magnifying glass

curtains

pot jug

book

leaf

steam

Cellophane sweet wrapper

cooking oil

used motor oil

window

sun visor

tin can

sunglasses

glass jug

plastic cup

milk

tea towel

china cup and saucer

plastic bag

wood

glass bottle

see through (transparent)

almost see through (translucent)

can't see through (opaque)

The Sun, Moon and Earth

Sun

Earth

Moon

Write in the missing words.

The ☀ is a big star.

We live on planet 🌍 .

The ☽ goes round the Earth.

Sun ☀	Moon ☽	Earth 🌍

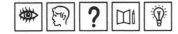

Why night occurs

We wanted to show why night occurs.

We used these things: _____

_____

This is what we did: _____

_____

_____

_____

_____

This is what we saw: _____

_____

Name _____

After school

Summer

In summer the sky is _____ when we go home from school.

Winter

In winter the sky is _____ when we go home from school.

Downy duckling's walk

Can you make the sounds of the things I saw?

Downy duckling walked out in the sunshine.

He saw a little bee on a flower.

He saw a grey cat washing his fur.

He saw a tree blown in the wind.

He saw a fire engine  in the road.

He saw a dog in a garden.

He saw raindrops falling on his nose.

He waddled quickly to the farmyard and
he saw his mum looking for him. So he hurried home.

"Quack quack", he said.

How I made a sound on this instrument

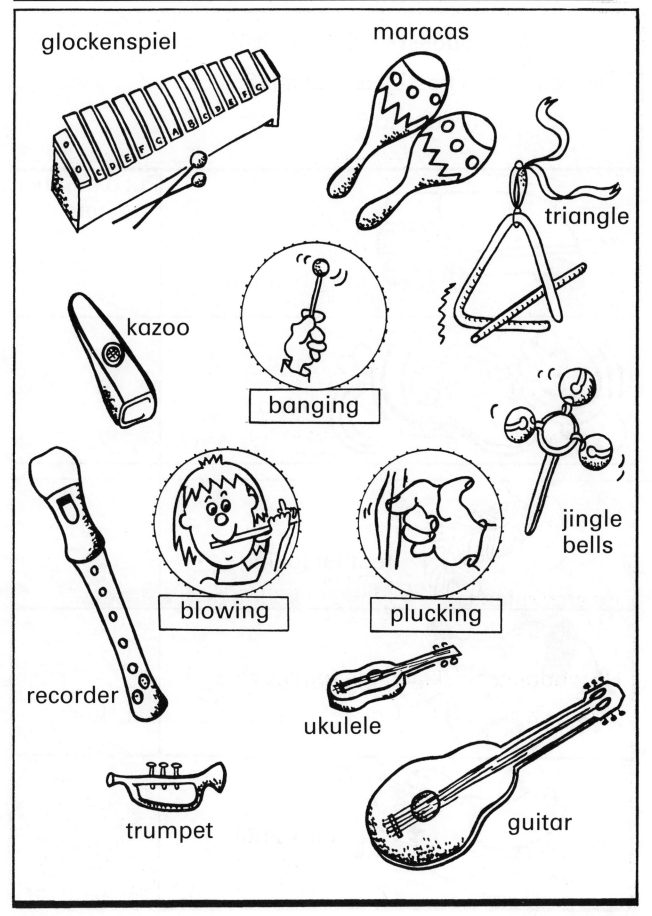

glockenspiel

maracas

triangle

kazoo

banging

blowing

plucking

jingle bells

recorder

ukulele

trumpet

guitar

Sounds

Which was loudest?   Number it 1.

Which was softest?   Number it 5.

Put them in order 1 to 5.

	Put a number here
lorry rushing	
wind	
feather falling	
dog barking	
bird singing	

Making sounds

How can you make sounds with these instruments?

tambourine	guitar
recorder	drum
claves	glockenspiel

shake	strike	pluck	blow	beat

Echo survey

Place	Surfaces	Echo		
		good	fair	poor

Hearing sounds

How well can you hear these things?

	close to	far away	in another room	with other noise
blowing recorder				
shouting				
radio				
talking				
beating drum				
spoon and glass				

Can hear	✓	Cannot hear	✗

Copymaster 95

Picking up sounds

♪♩ ♫♩♪♩♩ ♫♩♩	with ear cups	without
whistle	_____ metres	_____ metres
whisper	_____ metres	_____ metres
triangle	_____ metres	_____ metres
cymbals	_____ metres	_____ metres
shout	_____ metres	_____ metres

in front	behind	left side	right side

Copymaster 96

Sounds and materials

plastic bag

Type of box

_____

Material used

_____

Plasticine	newspaper	thick woolly jumper	tin foil
cotton wool	plastic bags	wood shavings	sand

What I did

What I discovered

RECORD SHEETS
1–6

Key Stage One: Experimental and investigative science
Level descriptions one & two

Name

Year/Class

A record of the number of experiences of experimental and investigative processes.

								👁
								🙂
								📏
								📖✏
								👄
								📊
								⚪
								⚠
								?
								🔍
								💡
								H
								🌀

RECORD SHEET 2

Key Stage One: Experimental and investigative science
Level description three

Name

Year/Class

A record of the number of experiences of experimental and investigative processes.

								👁
								🗣
								📏
								✏
								👄
								📊
								○
								🔍
								⚖
								H
								🌀
								123=
								💡
								⚠

RECORD SHEET 3

Key Stage One

Name

Level   **Year/Class**

Life processes and living things	
Materials and their properties	
Physical processes	

Comments

RECORD SHEET 4

Key Stage One

Name

Level   **Year/Class**

Life processes and living things

Comments

RECORD SHEET 5

Key Stage One

Name

Level   **Year/Class**

Materials and their properties

Comments

RECORD SHEET 6

Key Stage One

Name

Level

Year/Class

Physical processes

Comments